YOUR KNOWLEDGE HAS VALUE

- We will publish your bachelor's and master's thesis, essays and papers

- Your own eBook and book - sold worldwide in all relevant shops

- Earn money with each sale

Upload your text at www.GRIN.com
and publish for free

Bibliographic information published by the German National Library:

The German National Library lists this publication in the National Bibliography; detailed bibliographic data are available on the Internet at http://dnb.dnb.de .

This book is copyright material and must not be copied, reproduced, transferred, distributed, leased, licensed or publicly performed or used in any way except as specifically permitted in writing by the publishers, as allowed under the terms and conditions under which it was purchased or as strictly permitted by applicable copyright law. Any unauthorized distribution or use of this text may be a direct infringement of the author s and publisher s rights and those responsible may be liable in law accordingly.

Imprint:

Copyright © 2015 GRIN Verlag, Open Publishing GmbH
Print and binding: Books on Demand GmbH, Norderstedt Germany
ISBN: 9783668417137

This book at GRIN:

http://www.grin.com/en/e-book/356371/the-evolution-of-the-language-used-in-social-media

Nathan Heid

The Evolution of The Language Used In Social Media

GRIN Publishing

GRIN - Your knowledge has value

Since its foundation in 1998, GRIN has specialized in publishing academic texts by students, college teachers and other academics as e-book and printed book. The website www.grin.com is an ideal platform for presenting term papers, final papers, scientific essays, dissertations and specialist books.

Visit us on the internet:

http://www.grin.com/

http://www.facebook.com/grincom

http://www.twitter.com/grin_com

Nathan Heid

English Composition

4 December 2016

The Evolution of Language Used in Social Media

What is social media? Social media is any media of communication that allows users to create or share content with other people in their network. Over the past decade and a half, social media has grown in size and popularity. All over the world people are messaging each other through instant messaging applications like "Kik" and "Facebook Messenger", sending each other silly photos with dog ears and a dog nose with applications like "Snapchat", and tagging each other in various memes on Facebook and Instagram. With the recent introduction of social media, communicating with people has become easier than ever. With the push of a button, people can communicate with others across the globe in an instant. With the invention of social media, a new pseudo-language has been created ; using words like "LOL, ROFL, and, LMAO" and sayings like "Hit me up, what's the move?, and Sliding into the DM's", and sending Emojis such as "• ". All these words have different meaning now than they did 10 years. Ultimately, social media has changed how we as a society communicate in the modern age, but with the strengthened communication over the internet over the recent years, our face to face conversation skills have fallen short.

Many Americans speak in the English language but with social media, it is a whole different story. Social media sites like Facebook, Twitter, and Instagram have created a new language of their own. Words like *Avatar, Bio, Chat, and Follower* all have entirely new meanings behind them. Avatar used to be a Hindu term for a material manifestation of a deity. Bio used to be a detailed description of someone's life. Chat used to be just an informal conversation. Follower used to be a synonym for acolyte or companion. Now, avatar is a graphical representation of someone over the internet, bio's are short explainer texts on someone's profile, a witty little phrase, or a quote that they happen to enjoy, chats can refer to chat rooms where people will hang out in a virtual room and hold conversations, and follower refers to someone who subscribed to an entity on social media to receive updates from them. Many of these words are very similar to the definition of the words before the invention of social media but now they are modified to fit the needs for social media. Social Media has also created words of their own. Words like *Blog, Hashtag, Selfie, and Tweet.* These words have never existed before the invention of social media, but now with the introduction of social media these words are more prominent than ever.

    The way we communicate can change drastically just based on what the social media platform you are using is. For instance, Twitter limits their status updates or tweets to 140 text characters so users do not have a lot of space to convey what they want to. Unlike Facebook, which allows users to uses up to 60,000 characters. That means that Facebook's statuses allow over 430 times the amount of content that Twitter's tweets allow. That shows that twitter users are probably more likely to use shortened versions of their language to fit their needs for their form of social media. Compared to Facebook, which essentially does not limit its characters (it actually does but nobody will ever reach that character limit) on its status updates, the users of Facebook probably do not shorten what they are trying to say as much as a Twitter user would.

Another evolution in the language of social media is the usage of emojis and emoticons. Emoticons have been in use since the early days of the internet, before social media emerged. The usage of emoticons has been tracked back to the 19th century. The first usage of emoticons in the modern, digital age was by professor Scott Fahlman in 1982. On the computer science message board for Carnegie Mellon University, Professor Fahlman proposed to use ':-)'and ':-(' to distinguish jokes from more serious posts. Within a few months, the use of emoticons had become very popular, and the set of emoticons was extended with hugs and kisses, by using characters found on a typical keyboard. Almost a decade later, emoticons have found themselves in everyday communication over the internet.

Petra Kralj Novak, a researcher at the Department of Knowledge Technologies, writes "There is a new generation of emoticons, called emojis, that is increasingly being used in mobile communications and social media" (Novak et al 1). Emoji's have developed into a pseudo-language of it's own. Novak et al writes, "An emoji is a graphic symbol, ideogram, that represents not only facial expressions, but also concepts and ideas, such as celebration, weather, vehicles and buildings, food and drink, animals and plants, or emotions, feelings, and activities" (Novak et al 1). Emojis are used on a daily basis on almost all social media sites. In the last two years, there have been over 10,000,000,000 emojis used on twitter alone. Emoji's may just be emoticons in a new form but the recent usage of emoji's over social media has developed them into a new pseudo-language of their own. Emojis could be used to to convey emotions and feelings. Emojis can be considered the equivalent to someone facial expressions. People who use social media frequently will often be able to understand strings of emojis in conversation as an alternative to using written words.

Emojis are frequently used in texting and text conversations. Texting is a social media form of it's own. Texting is a form of social media known as "Direct Messaging". Text messages are also known as SMS messages. Erika M. Patterson, a Professor at Winthrop University writes, "Text messaging consists of 140 bytes of information available in each message sent. The Oxford English Dictionary Online defines SMS, or "short message service, a digital communication system enabling mobile phones to send and receive short text messages" (Patterson 1). When texting was in it's infant stages the amount of data that could be sent was very limited. People had to use shorthand for messages that they were going to send because of the limited data amount. For example, sending *Txt* instead of text, *b4* instead of before. This style of speaking is known as text speak.

Text speak is a shorthand version of english. Some people try to argue that texting and using text-speak causes illiteracy in young people. Patterson disagrees with this idea. Patterson writes,

> Therefore, even with the incorporation of a foreign language, our native language of Standard English and its correct grammatical uses would not be forgotten by children beyond a the ages of six or seven, since our native language, linguistic sounds and patterns, and grammatical uses are hardwired by then and text speak would not affect our already developed patterns in linguistics. (Patterson 240-241)

Even though young people are constantly using textspeak, Paterson believes that text speak is not to blame for illiteracy in young people. People learned how to use grammar properly in their younger days. Using text speak would not just erase everything that people have learned in their younger years. With the introduction of texting and direct messaging social media, the usage of acronyms has skyrocketed. Words like *LOL, ROFL, LMAO, and, OMG* all have their definitions but now they have evolved into something completely different. Even in the short time that texting has been around there have been evolutions within the texting language. John McWhorter, an American linguist said, "LOL does not mean Laugh out Loud anymore, It's evolved into something a lot subtler" (McWhorter). People will just use words like "Lol" or "Rofl" as a pragmatic particle: a word used to fill in gaps in discourse. Words like LOL and ROFL are rarely used in their literal sense anymore.

With the internet so accessible, anybody and everybody has access to social media. This has led to a new type of bullying called Cyberbullying. Cyberbullying is just like any other bullying, one person or a group of people are the victim, and one or a group of people are the bullies. Cyber-bullying has been the topic of many debates revolving around social media. Cyber-bullying is so easy to do because how easy access there is to the internet and social media. One of the terms for a cyber-bully is a keyboard warrior. Some people think that they are invulnerable just because they are behind a computer monitor or a phone screen. People think they can just belittle others with no repercussions but there are repercussions. Some just can't handle the things that other people say to them. Cyber-bullying has been one of the largest causes of suicide since the age of social media has started.

Our face-to-face communication has weakened over the past decade due to the overuse of social media. A lot of people who frequently use social media are really bad at face to face conversations. It is easy to talk to someone over a screen but it is leagues more difficult to talk to someone face to face. A lot of people who use social media chose to use it in unhealthy ways. Stephen Krause, an English professor at the Eastern Michigan University, who studies the intersection between writing and technology. Krause writes, "If you turn to social media instead of instead of playing football, that's unhealthy" (Krause 149). Social media should be used to strengthen your face to face interactions by using it to your advantage. There are some people who will chose social media over face-to-face interactions and communications. That is one of the most unhealthy uses of social media.

Social media is one most useful tools invented over the last few decades. Social media has allowed people to connect with others far and wide; to rekindle old friendships and to build new ones. Social media has allowed people to speak their own opinions about certain topics with ease and build social groups that agree with those opinions, but with the easy access to social media comes peoples face to face sociability. People who frequently use social media often have trouble with face to face encounters.

Glossary

Avatar- An avatar is a graphical representation used to represent someone on a social media site.

Bio- Short for biography, is a short bit of text in someone's social media profile used to give a brief description of themself

Chat- Chat can refer to any type of communication over the internet but in the traditional sense refers to one-to-one communication over a text based application.

Cyber-bullying- Bullying done over the internet.

Direct Message- Also referred to as "DM", is a private exchange of messages over a social media site, usually twitter.

Emoticon- shorthand for a facial expression, Usually made with type symbols

Follower- refers to a person who subscribes to your account in order to receive your updates.

Hashtag- A hashtag is a tag used on a variety of social networks as a way to group posts and updates. Social networks use hashtags to categorize information and make it easily searchable for users.

Keyboard Warrior- Someone who says bullshit over the internet but is too big of a coward to say it in a face to face conflict.

Kik- An instant Messaging application

Like or Favorite- an action that can be made by on a social media site. Instead of writing a comment or sharing a post, a user can click the Like button as a quick way to show approval or that they acknowledged the post.

LOL- Laughing out loud; More often used as a pragmatic particle.

Meme- used to describe a thought, idea, joke, or concept that's widely shared online.

OMG- Oh my god/gosh

ROFL- Roll on floor laughing; used as a pragmatic particle

Snapchat- A photo messaging app that allows you to send videos and pictures with captions that will self destruct in 10 seconds after opening.

Selfie- A photograph that one has taken of oneself, typically one taken with a smartphone or webcam and shared via social media

Status- a posting on a social networking website that indicates a user's current situation, state of mind, or opinion about something.

Troll- a person who sows discord on the Internet by starting arguments or upsetting people

Tweet- A message sent through twitter; The verb used for posting messages on twitter

Works Cited

Gleick, James. "Living Within Social Networks". *Culture: A Reader for Writers*, Edited by John Mauk, Oxford University Press, 2014, PP.146-149

McWhorter, John. "Txting is Killing Language. JK!!!" *Ted.* Feb. 2013

Kralj Novak, Petra, et al. "Sentiment of Emojis." *PloS One.* Vol. 10 Issue 12. 2015. PP 1-22 doi: 10.1371/journal.pone.0144296.

Patterson, Erika. "Texting: an Old Habit in a New Media". *International Journal of The Humanities.* Vol. 9 Issue 7. 2011. Pp 235-242

YOUR KNOWLEDGE HAS VALUE

- We will publish your bachelor's and master's thesis, essays and papers

- Your own eBook and book - sold worldwide in all relevant shops

- Earn money with each sale

Upload your text at www.GRIN.com
and publish for free